ADVANCED VIOLA SCALE STUDIES

I0800330

ELAINE FINE

MEL BAY

WWW.MELBAY.COM

Introduction

Practicing scales is vital for building and maintaining technique. Through practicing scales we learn to navigate the fingerboard, shift from position to position, develop bow control, improve intonation, develop strength, and develop a vibrant and varied sound.

We all approach the practice of scales with the best of intentions, but at some point in the process, particularly when scales begin and end on the tonic note and ascend and descend with proscribed fingerings and bowing patterns, we may shut off our ears and minds and play automatically. While it is possible to develop strength, agility, and muscle memory through automatic scale playing, it is very easy to spend time playing through scales without being intellectually or musically engaged, and not really pay attention to the way different keys feel and sound on the viola, or even to what particular scale we happen to be playing.

The pieces in this book are musically, intellectually, and rhythmically challenging one-page lyrical compositions that move stepwise through each of the major and minor keys. The first 24 follow the circle of fifths, with the minor scale preceding its relative major. Everything moves stepwise, with pitches repeated at pitch level and at the octave. The stepwise motion and octave jumps makes navigation from one pitch to the next easy to hear, even when playing in keys with many sharps or flats.

Each piece is named for an animal that has scales. The pieces for the three squirrels use the same musical material in different keys. The members of the snake, crocodile, butterfly, fish, bird, lizard, and pangolin families share material, but employ a lot of variation. The butterflies all use a *tresillo* rhythm that divides the 8/8 meter into asymmetrical groups of threes and twos.

There are occasional indications of which string a passage should be played on, but I have left the fingering choices to the violist (or the teacher). There are no metronome markings indicated, only Italian (and sometimes English) suggestions of character. These pieces can be practiced at comfortable tempos with a metronome, but as solo concert pieces they should be played with expressive freedom.

I hope that practicing these pieces and learning about these animals will spark the creative imaginations of those who play them, and as people become more engaged with the expressive musical qualities that scales have to offer, they might be inspired to write scale pieces of their own.

Elaine Fine

Contents

Red-Tailed Boa

Boa constrictor

A minor

Mysterioso

Green Iguana

Iguana iguana

C major

Allegretto

Saw-Scaled Viper

Anilius scytale

E minor

Red Factor Canary

Serinius carnria domestica

G major

(LH pizz. on lower pitch only.)

Funereal Dusky-Wing Butterfly

Erynnis funeralis

B minor

Somber

American Crocodile

Crocodylus acutus

D major

Gorgon Copper Butterfly

Lycaena gorgono

F-sharp minor

Stellar's Sea Eagle

Haliaeetus pelagicus

A major

Lembert's Green Haristreak

Callophrys sherindanii lemberti

C-sharp minor

Lord Darby's Scaly-Tailed Squirrel

Anomalurus derebianus

E major

Allegro

Giant Pangolin

Smutsia gigantea

G-sharp minor

Freshwater Crocodile

Crocodylus jonsoni

B major

This can also be played half a step lower in B-flat major by replacing the sharps in the key signature with two flats.

Blowfish

Diodon antennatus

D-sharp minor

Cuban Crocodile

Crocodylus rhombifer

F-sharp major

Try it in F major as well. Just remove the sharps and add a single B-flat.

Rainbow Sardine

Dussumieria acuta

B-flat minor

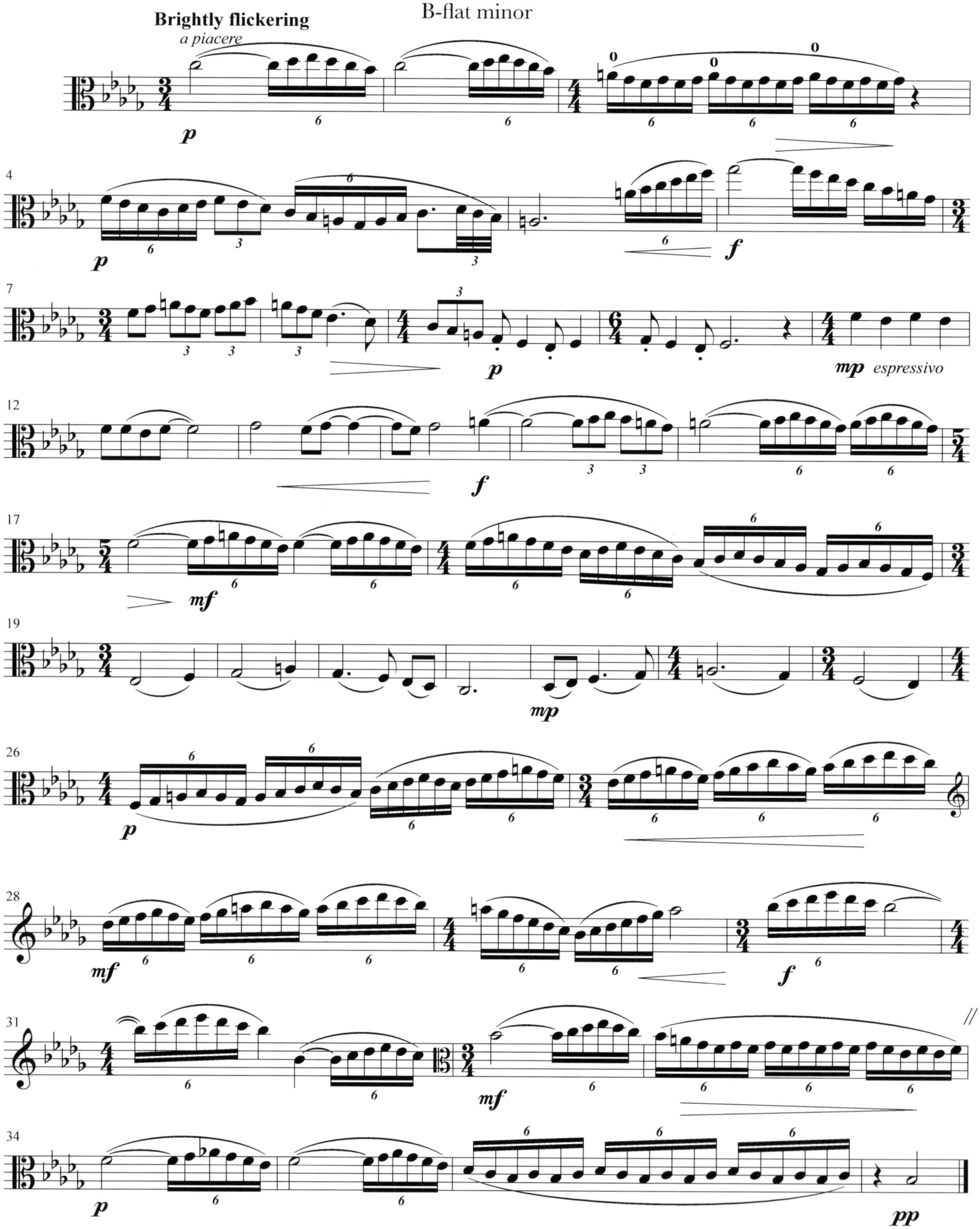

Musky Rat-Kangaroo

Hypsiprymnodon moschatus

D-flat major

Allegro

This can also be played in D major by replacing the four flats in the key signature with two sharps.

Great White Shark

Carcharoden Carcharias

F minor

Agitato

Blue Scaled Quail

Callipepla squamata

A-flat major

Brahminy Blind Snake

Indotyphlops braminus

C minor

Tokay Gecko

Gekko gecko

E-flat major

Neon Damselfish

Pomacentrus coelestis

G minor

Quasi sarabande

Pel's Flying Squirrel

Anomalurus pelii

B-flat major

Allegro

Cloudless Sulphur Butterfly

Phoebis sennae

D minor

Cameroon Scaly Tail Squirrel

Zenkerella insignis

F major

Sanford's Sea Eagle

Haliaeetus sanfordi

A-flat major

False Coral Snake

Anilius scytale

D minor

Black-Bellied Pangolin

Phataginus tetradactyla

G minor

Round Sardinella

Sardinella aurita

B-flat major

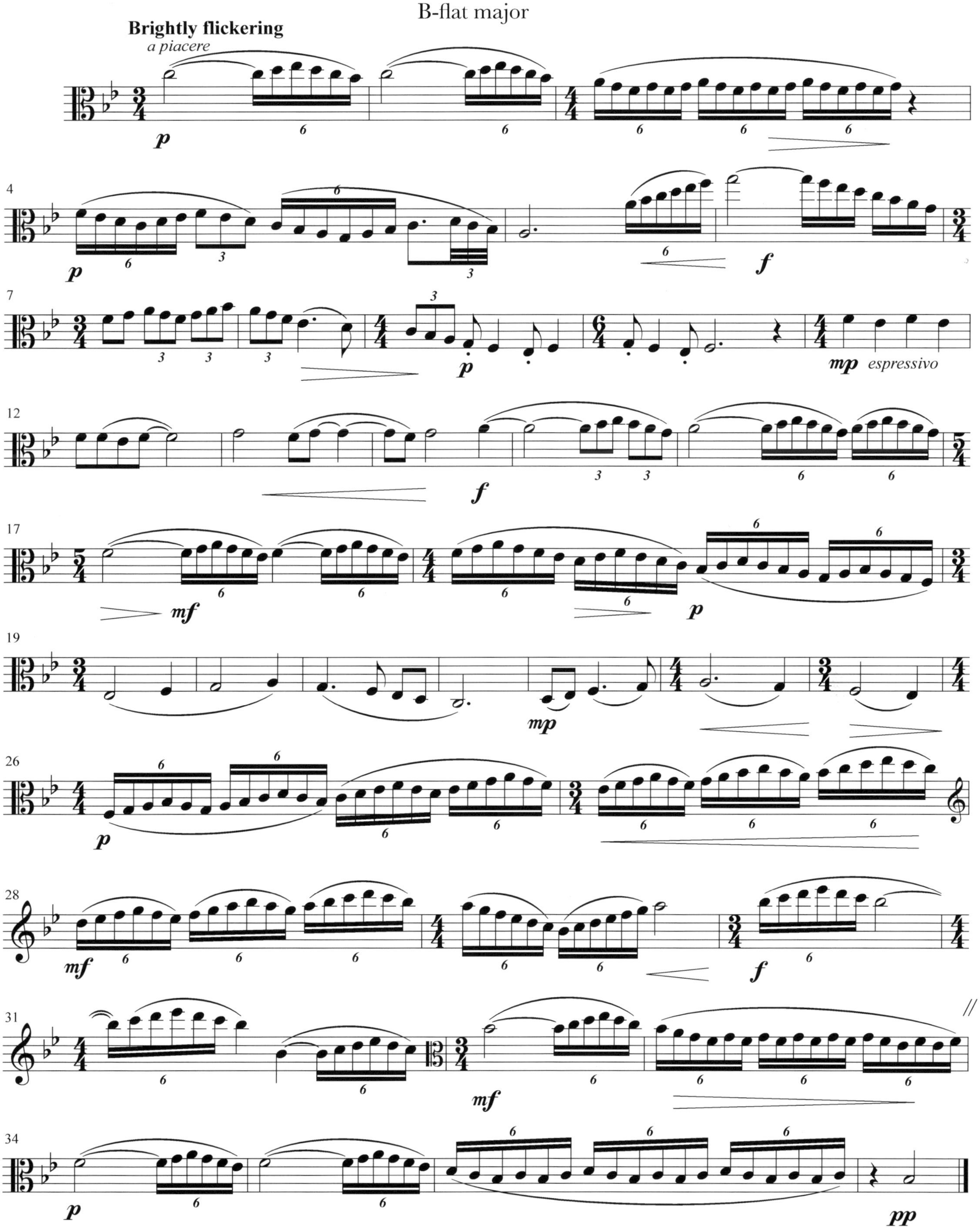

Northern Bobwhite

Colinus virginianus

A major